Descriptive text by Barbara Newson

Colourful Wales

Jarrold Colour Publications, Norwich

The Afon Goedol (1) near Blaenau Ffestiniog, Merionethshire.
La Rivière Goedol (1) près de Blaenau Ffestiniog dans le Merionethshire.
Der Afon Goedol (1) bei Blaenau Ffestiniog, Grafschaft Merioneth.

North Wales

Just a short journey from busy industrial England the land of North Wales offers a complete change of scene and way of life. This is a land of great and varied beauty, a land of contrasts and a land with a long history. Primarily a region of mountains and rugged splendour, it has been the scene of grim historic battles, and the chain of fortresses established by Edward I from Flint to Cardigan Bay bears testimony of the hard struggle. Among the peaks of Snowdonia are the highest mountains in England and Wales. In the past these acted as a natural and invincible fortress from which the Welsh launched their attacks on invading armies. Protected now as a National Park, this is an area of grandeur, magnificent mountain peaks, fast-flowing rivers, and beautiful lakes. Legend is as strong as history in the Welsh mountains and this region is associated with the greatest legends of Vortigern, Merlin and Arthur and his knights.

North Wales does not consist solely of rugged mountains, however. Within a few miles you will find scenery of a softer nature: fertile valleys, deep winding rivers, estuaries and lakes, moors, great forests and beautiful villages packed with interest. The Isle of Anglesey, called the 'Mother of Wales' because she was the national granary, offers the quiet beauty of rich pastures, while the coastline of North Wales offers a variety of scenery and pleasant resorts. There are always dramatic sights to be enjoyed of mountain, land and sea, of magnificent waterfalls, and sometimes even of semitropical flowers growing within view of snow-capped mountain peaks.

Despite its quarries and mines, and the light industries which have been established to combat growing unemployment, the character of North Wales remains predominantly rural, with a high percentage of the population earning their living from the land. The next most important industry is tourism, with a greater number of visitors each year coming to enjoy the variety and beauty which North Wales has to offer.

2

3

4

Le Château Hawarden (2) dans le Flint longe la route principale de Chester à la côte nord du Pays de Galles. Ce château fut construit en 1752, et au 19e siècle il devint la demeure de Gladstone. Au nord-ouest de Hawarden, à côté de la Rivière Clwyd, se trouve le Château de Rhuddlan (3) qui date du 13e siècle. A l'embouchure de la Clwyd est située Rhyl (4), station balnéaire populaire, et plus à l'ouest, Llandudno (7). Le Grand Orme, promontoire qui protège cette ville sur son côté nord-ouest peut être remonté par ascenseur (5). Sur ses pentes sud on voit les Jardins Haulfre (6).

Schloß Hawarden bei Flint (2) steht dicht an der Hauptstraße von Chester nach der Küste von Nordwales. Dieses Schloß wurde 1752 gebaut und im 19. Jahrhundert ging es in den Besitz des Staatsmannes Gladstone über. Nordwestlich von Hawarden am Fluß Clwyd steht Schloß Rhuddlan (3), das aus dem 13. Jahrhundert stammt. An der Mündung des Clwyd befindet sich das beliebte Seebad Rhyl (4), und weiter östlich liegt Llandudno (7). Kap Great Orme, das die nordwestliche Flanke dieser Stadt schützt, kann mit einer Luftseilbahn (5) erreicht werden. Auf seinen Hängen sind die Haulfre Gärten (6).

Many visitors to Wales are particularly attracted by the combination of land, sea and mountain which the many pleasant resorts of the northern coastline have to offer. Every year these resorts welcome more and more holidaymakers, especially from the North and the Midlands for whom Prestatyn, Rhyl, Colwyn Bay and Llandudno have an especially strong appeal. Visitors making their way towards the north coast by the main road from Chester pass close by Hawarden Castle (2) built in 1752. In the nineteenth century this castle was inherited by Catherine Glynne, who in 1839 married the statesman Gladstone. The castle became Gladstone's home and remained so for sixty years. North-west of Hawarden beside the Clwyd River stand the superb ruins of Rhuddlan Castle (3). These ruins date from the thirteenth century when the castle was built by Edward I as one of a stronghold chain to control North Wales.

North of Rhuddlan on the mouth of the Clwyd is the popular seaside resort of Rhyl (4). Since the early nineteenth century it has grown from a small fishing village into a large modern resort with every facility for a memorable holiday. These include a two-mile-long promenade and great expanses of magnificent beaches. Further west is Colwyn Bay. Situated on a wide bay sheltered by Penmaen Head, it enjoys a mild climate. Still further west along this coast is Llandudno (7), which occupies a superb position on the narrow isthmus east of the Conway estuary. The town is in many respects unusual, for in the mid-nineteenth century it was systematically planned and laid out as a pleasure resort by Lord Mostyn. Llandudno has two sea fronts; one runs along the wide sweep of its eastern bay between the Great and Little Ormes while the western front faces Conway Bay. The Great Orme, which shelters the town on its north-western flank, is encircled by a fine marine drive four miles in length, and may be ascended by a cabin lift (5). On the head of the Great Orme stands a tiny chapel, dedicated to St Tudno, from whom the town gets its name, and on its southern slopes are the Haulfre Gardens (6) where many subtropical flowers grow.

5

7

6

The ancient town of Conway (8) stands at the head of the estuary of the River Conway. Edward I built the massive castle as part of his stronghold chain to control North Wales, and surrounded the town of Conway with stout walls. Although Conway Castle is a ruin, much of its masonry has withstood the ravages of time. The castle is oblong in form, with walls at least fifteen feet thick and flanked by eight huge circular towers. The main road from Conway to Bangor runs along the coast, but inland there is a less frequented route with impressive scenery over the Sychnant Pass (9), which descends to join the coast at Penmaenmawr. From here the road follows the coast to Bangor, a cathedral and university city on the southern shore of the Menai Strait (10). The Menai Strait separates the island of Anglesey from the mainland of North Wales, and is spanned by the graceful suspension bridge for road traffic and the Britannia Tubular Bridge which carries the main railway line. Anglesey is renowned for its long history and the peaceful beauty of its rich pastures. At its northern extremity stands Penmon Priory (11), founded in the sixth century by St Seiriol, and much later rebuilt as an Augustinian monastery. The church is beautifully restored and contains some fine Norman work. Back on the mainland the town of Caernarvon stands just within the western entrance to the Menai Strait. Caernarvon Castle (12), one of the finest in the British Isles, was begun in the thirteenth century by Edward I and completed by his son. It covers three acres and impresses from every viewpoint.

9

10

Le Château de Conway (8) dans le Caernarvonshire, en tête de la Rivière Conway, fut construit par Edward I. La grand-route de Conway à Bangor longe la côte, mais il y a une route alternative par le Sychnant Pass (9) qui traverse un paysage intérieur impressionnant. Le Menai Strait (10) sépare l'île d'Anglesey des terres du nord du Pays de Galles. A l'extrémité nord-est d'Anglesey se trouve le Prieuré de Penmon (11) fondé au 6e siècle. Le Château de Caernarvon (12), un des plus beaux châteaux des Iles Britanniques remonte au 13e siècle. Il couvre plus d'un hectare.

Schloß Conway (8), Grafschaft Caernarvon, das an der Quelle des Conway steht, wurde von Eduard dem Ersten gebaut. Die Hauptstraße von Conway nach Bangor folgt der Küste, aber es gibt eine zweite Straße, die über den Sychnantpaß (9) und durch eine eindrucksvolle Binnenlandschaft führt. Die Menai-Straße (10) trennt die Insel Anglesey vom Festland. An der nordöstlichen Spitze von Anglesey steht die Probstei Penmon (11), die ursprünglich im 6. Jahrhundert gegründet wurde. Schloß Caernarvon (12), eines der schönsten Schlösser der Britischen Inseln, stammt aus dem 13. Jahrhundert.

11

12

13

Telford's famous route to Holyhead through the heart of North Wales enters Caernarvonshire at Betws-y-coed (14). This village, whose name means 'the chapel in the wood', enjoys a beautiful setting where the valleys of the Conway and the Llugwy meet. It is claimed to be 'the beauty spot of Wales' and certainly is an enchanting place with much of interest. The old church contains a Norman font and the grave effigy of Gruffyd, son of Dafydd the Red and grand-nephew of Llewelyn ap Gruffyd. The four-arched bridge, called Pont-y-Pair, across the Llugwy carries the Llanwryst road and dates from the fifteenth century. The main road crosses the Conway over Waterloo Bridge, which dates from 1815. Another notable bridge is the wooden Miners' Bridge over the Llugwy, built to enable the miners of Pentre-Du to reach their work on the opposite bank. Betws-y-coed is famous for the three fine waterfalls in its vicinity. One of these is the Swallow Falls (15) on the River Llugwy, where the stream of the river hurrying down from the mountains is broken into numerous cascades by jagged rocks. The others are the Conway Falls on the Conway River and the Pandy Falls on the River Machno. Another much visited spot in the vicinity is the Fairy Glen, a delightful place where rocks and trees tower above the rushing stream.

A few miles south-east of Betws-y-coed is the charming hamlet of Capel Garmon (13) among trees and hills. Close to this hamlet is Capel Garmon Cromlech, an ancient monument which consists of burial chambers probably dating from the Bronze Age. This spot is immensely interesting archaeologically and also provides splendid westward views. South-west of Betws-y-coed in the picturesque valley of the Lledr lies the village of Dolwyddelan, once very involved with the slate-quarrying industry which has now declined. The village has a church dating from the sixteenth century and about a mile from the village the remains of a rugged castle (16), possibly dating from the twelfth century. It is said that Llewelyn the Great, who reigned from 1194 to 1240, was born here.

Betws-y-coed (14) profite d'une situation splendide, à l'encontre des vallées de Conway et de Llugwy. A quelques milles au sud-est se trouve Capel Garmon (13) connu pour son « Cromlech », série de chambres mortuaires qui datent probablement de l'âge de bronze. Dans le voisinage de Betws-y-coed on trouve de nombreuses attractions, parmi lesquelles les Chutes des Hirondelles (15) sur la Rivière Machno. Au sud-ouest de Betws-y-coed est le village de Dolwyddelan. On dit que le Château de Dolwyddelan (16), qui date probablement du 12e siècle, est le lieu de naissance de Llewelyn le Grand.

Betws-y-coed (14) genießt eine wunderschöne Lage, wo das Conwaytal und das Llugwytal zusammentreffen. Einige Meilen südöstlich befindet sich Capel Garmon (13), berühmt wegen seiner „Cromlech" – einer Anzahl Grüfte, die wahrscheinlich aus dem Bronzezeitalter stamen. In der Umgebung von Betws-y-coed sind zahlreiche Sehenswürdigkeiten, darunter der Schwalbenfall (15) am Fluß Machno. Südwestlich von Betws-y-coed liegt das Dorf Dolwyddelan. Schloß Dolwyddelan (16), das möglicherweise aus dem 12. Jahrhundert stammt, soll der Geburtsort von Llewelyn dem Großen sein.

14

15

16

17

18

19

Au-delà de Capel Curig on peut voir les hauteurs de Gallt-yr-Ogof, au sud desquelles coule la Rivière Nant-y-Gors (17). Llyn Ogwen (18) à l'extrême sud de la Passe du Nant Ffrancon est bien connue par les pêcheurs pour ses truites et ses anguilles; et du désert Llyn Mymbyr (19) au sud du Llyn Ogwen, on a des vues splendides sur les Snowdon. Au nord-ouest coule la tumultueuse Rivière Seiont vers Llyn Padarn (20), qui a deux milles de long et qui suit au sud-est les contours des Snowdon.

Jenseits Capel Curig kann man den Gipfel von Gallt-yr-Ogof sehen, und südlich davon fließt der Nant-y-Gors (17). Llyn Ogwen (18), am südlichen Ende des Nant Ffrancon-Passes, ist unter Anglern wegen seiner Forellen und Aalen berühmt, und vom abgelegenen Llyn Mymbyr (19), südlich des Llyn Ogwen, genießt man eine schöne Aussicht auf den Snowdon. Nordwestlich davon fließt der reißende Wildbach Seiont gegen den Llyn Padarn (20), der zwei Meilen lang ist.

Six miles to the west of Betws-y-coed is Capel Curig, a village beautifully situated at the junction of the main road to Bangor and Holyhead and the road to Beddgelert. It takes its name from St Curig, a British recluse who came to the spot in the sixth century, and to whom the church is dedicated. Capel Curig, standing at about 600 feet and overlooked by the hills of Moel Siabod and Pen Llithrig-y-Wrach, is renowed for its bracing air. It is a noted angling centre and is a popular base among hill-walkers, for it is within easy reach of Carneddau, the Glyders and Snowdon.

From Capel Curig the road to Bangor rises steadily, passing through magnificent scenery. Along the route are to be seen the heights of Gallt-yr-Ogof, whose name means 'the cavernous cliffs', with the stream of Nant-y-Gors flowing beneath it (17). Some seven miles beyond this the road reaches a height of a thousand feet as it runs between the noble mountain Tryfan (3,010 feet) and Llyn Ogwen (18). Tryfan is shaped like a pyramid, and with its varied and pinnacled rockwork is a paradise for expert climbers. Llyn Ogwen is set in a deep hollow on the slopes of Tryfan and is famous for its trout and eels. Near Ogwen Bridge are two romantic spots. One of these is Llyn Idwal, over which according to legend no bird dare fly; and the other is a depression in the mountainside known as the 'Devil's Kitchen'. At the western end of Llyn Ogwen the road descends to cross the wildly beautiful Nant Ffrancon Pass ('the Vale of Beavers'), a rugged natural amphitheatre which was once the bed of a glacier. The old road, now a grassy track, has been superseded by the modern highway.

The road from Capel Curig to Beddgelert ascends Nant-y-Gwryd passing close to Llyn Mymbyr (19), one of the many lakes of Snowdonia and good for trout fishing. Here in this isolated spot there are fine views of Snowdon to be had. The road continues, reaching Pen-y-Gwryd, a hotel opened in 1847 and well known to climbers as 'Pyg'. Here there is a choice of route, south-west to Beddgelert or north-west over the Pass of Llanberis towards Caernarvon, following the course of the turbulent River Seiont as it hurries towards Llyn Peris and Llyn Padarn (20). Llyn Peris is about one mile long while Llyn Padarn is two miles long and framed on the south-east by the bold contours of Snowdon. Between the two lakes is the terminus of the Snowdon Mountain Railway, opened in 1896, the only one of its kind in the British Isles. The line is nearly five miles long and the journey to the summit takes an hour.

20

21

22

Le sommet le plus haut des Snowdon est le Y Wyddfa. Il peut être monté à pied ou par le chemin de fer de montagne des Snowdon (22). D'en haut la vue sur Llyn Llydaw (21) est splendide de même d'ailleurs que la vue des Snowdon à partir du Llyn Llydaw (23). De Llanberis, au pied des Snowdon, la Passe de Llanberis (24) atteint une hauteur de milles pieds au-dessus du niveau de la mer. A Pen-y-Gwryd c'est par un tournant à droite que commence la descente du Nant Gwynant le long de la vallée du Glaslyn. Nant Gwynant est surveillé par Moel Hebog (25), dont le nom veut dire « La Colline du Faucon ». Llyn Gwynant (26) se trouve dans un beau paysage.

Snowdons höhster Gipfel heißt Y Wyddfa; man kann ihn zu Fuß besteigen oder mit der Snowdon-Bergbahn (22) fahren. Die Aussicht vom Gipfel über Llyn Llydaw (21) ist wunderschön, wie auch diejenige auf Snowdon von Llyn Llydaw (23). Von Llanberis am Fuße des Snowdon steigt der Llanberispaß (24) zu einer Höhe von über 1000 Fuß ü.M. Bei Pen-y-Gwryd beginnt sich das Glaslyntal langsam zu senken, durchfloßen vom Nant Gwynant. Nant Gwynant wird vom Moel Hebog (25) überragt, wo sich Owen Glendower verborgen haben soll, als ihn die Englander verfolgten. Llyn Gwynant (26) befindet sich inmitten einer wunderschönen Landschaft.

23

24

25

Snowdon, well known as the highest mountain in England and Wales, actually has five peaks. Only the highest, which is known as Y Wyddfa and is 3,560 feet above sea level, qualifies for the title of 'Snowdon'. The others are known as Crib-y-Ddysgl, Crib Goch, Lliwedd and Yr Aran. Among this mountain mass five great cwms or hollows have been carved out, and nestling in these are fine lakes, each with its own particular charm to add to Snowdonia's scenic splendour. The lake below Y Wyddfa is Llyn Llydaw (23). Snowdon belies its name, for its summit (21) is well below the snow-line, although the snow which has fallen in winter often persists until late spring. Visitors find that although Snowdon offers good climbing and walking, it is not difficult to conquer, and the tracks to the summit are generally well marked and safe. Of the seven or eight recognised routes the easiest ascent is by way of the bridle path from Llanberis, a route which for the most part follows the mountain railway. Many, of course, prefer to travel by this unusual railway (22) and enjoy extensive views as the train approaches the summit. On a clear day the views extend as far as the Isle of Man, the Cumberland Mountains and even to Ireland.

From Llanberis, at the foot of Snowdon, the Pass of Llanberis (24) climbs to a height of over 1,000 feet above sea level and is undoubtedly one of the most impressive roads in the country. At Pen-y-Gwryd a right turn begins the descent of Nant Gwynant (25) along the valley of the Glaslyn, with fine views of the southern slopes of the Snowdon range, especially from the vicinity of Lake Gwynant (26).

Llyn Dinas (27), au nord-est de Beddgelert, est connu pour sa beauté et son association avec la légende de Vortigern, un gouverneur de Grande-Bretagne. De Llyn Dinas le fleuve Glaslyn coule vers Beddgelert, surveillé par Dinas Emrys (28), le « Fort d'Emrys ». Le charmant petit village de Beddgelert (29) se trouve au confluent des rivières Colwyn et Glaslyn et est surmonté par Moel Hebog. Au sud de Beddgelert le fleuve Glaslyn coule à travers la célèbre Passe de Aberglaslyn (30). Au delà de la Passe le Glaslyn (31) coule à travers un pays moins austère en direction du sud. Vue du pont Tan-lan la montagne Cnicht (32) apparaît en un pic pointu et a été surnommé le « Mont Cervin » du Pays de Galles.

Llyn Dinas (27), nordöstlich von Beddgelert, ist wegen seinem Reiz berühmt und wird ferner in Verbindung gebracht mit der Sage des Vortigern, einer der Könige Britanniens. Von Llyn Dinas fließt der Afon Glaslyn weiter gegen Beddgelert, von der Dinas Emrys (28) überblickt. Das reizende kleine Dorf Beddgelert (29) steht am Zusammenfluß des Colwyn und des Glaslyn und wird vom Moel Hebog überblickt. Südlich von Beddgelert fließt der Glaslyn durch den berühmten Aberglaslynpaß (30). Jenseits des Passes fließt der Glaslyn (31) nach Süden. Von der Brücke Tan-lan aus gesehen, erscheint der Cnichtberg (32) als ein scharfer Gipfel, den man schon das walisische Matterhorn genannt hat.

27

28

29

30

31

32

Beyond Lake Gwynant in the direction of Beddgelert lies Llyn Dinas (27), famous for its beauty and also its association with the legend of Vortigern. From Lake Gwynant the Afon Glaslyn continues its descent of the wooded valley. On its right bank rises Dinas Emrys (28), a hill associated with Geoffrey of Monmouth's Arthurian legend. It is said that Dinas Emrys ('fort of Emrys') was granted by Vortigern, a ruler of Britain, to the great Merlin, called Emrys, who was probably one of the commanders of Vortigern's forces. The village of Beddgelert (29) stands at the junction of two deep river valleys, where the Glaslyn and the Colwyn flow into one another. There is more than one theory as to how it received its name. One says that the name means 'grave of Gelert', derived from a legend of Llewelyn the Great and his hound Gelert. This legend says that while Llewelyn was out hunting he used to leave his infant son in the care of his hound Gelert. One day he returned to find the boy's cradle overturned and thinking that Gelert had killed his son he slew the dog. Only then did he find his son unharmed and a dead wolf to testify to the faithfulness of Gelert. There is, however, no historical evidence to support this story. Another theory suggests that perhaps the village took its name from a St Kelert and time and usage distorted this to the present name.

However it came by its name, the village is charming. It is a very popular centre for Snowdonia and is a favourite haunt of artists and photographers. Above the village rises Moel Hebog, 'the hill of the hawk'. Beddgelert is the starting point for many fine walks, one of the most rewarding being through the Pass of Aberglaslyn (30). This is a gorge, rather than a pass, through which the River Glaslyn tumbles. Beyond the pass the Glaslyn (31) flows through less rugged country on its journey southwards. At some distance east of Beddgelert the mountain Cnicht (2,265 feet) rises majestically and offers interesting climbing. Viewed from Tan-lan bridge (32), it appears a sharp peak and has been called the Welsh Matterhorn.

33

34

35

36

Le campagne des alentours de Ffestiniog offre de charmantes promenades montagneuses, telle l'ascension du Moelwyn Bach (33), tandis que les Chutes de Cymerau (34), à environ un demi-mille de Ffestiniog constituent un spectacle splendide. La Vallée de Ffestiniog (35) devint d'abord célèbre grâce aux carrières d'ardoise de Blaenau Ffestiniog, mais elle est de nos jours renommée pour sa splendide beauté. Portmadoc (36) est un petit centre d'affaires construit au 19e siècle à l'estuaire de la Glaslyn. Portmeirion (37) est un village des plus insolites du Pays de Galles car il est tout à fait de style italien.

Die Landschaft um Ffestiniog bietet entzückende Bergwanderungen, darunter die Besteigung des Moelwyn Bach (33), während der Cymeraufall (34) – ungefähr eine halbe Meile von Ffestiniog entfernt – einen prächtigen Anblick bietet. Das Ffestiniogtal (35) wurde durch die Ausbeutung seiner Schieferbrüche bei Blaenau Ffestiniog bekannt, ist aber jetzt hauptsächlich wegen seinem natürlichen Reiz berühmt. Portmadoc (36) ist eine Handelsstadt, die im 19. Jahrhundert gebaut wurde. Portmeirion (37) ist das ungewöhnlichste Dorf von ganz Wales, denn es ist ganz im italienischen Stil gebaut.

The Vale of Ffestiniog (35), Merionethshire, became famous for the slate-quarrying carried out at Blaenau Ffestiniog, but has won praise for its beauty. Through the wooded, steep-sided vale flows the River Dwyd and along the western edge is the Ffestiniog Railway track, originally built to carry slates from the Blaenau Ffestiniog quarries to Portmadoc (36) for shipment. At the vale's head nestles the very attractive village of Ffestiniog. This village offers delightful mountain walks, including the ascent of Moelwyn Bach (33), and there are several lakes offering good fishing. Also in the vicinity are a number of waterfalls which are worth visiting, including the beautiful Cymerau Falls (34), where the waters flow between moss-covered rocks, and the Cynfal Falls, noted for their tall rock column, known as Hugh Lloyd's Pulpit. This is said to have been used in magical practices of the sixteenth century.

Portmadoc, Caernarvonshire, on the beautiful Glaslyn estuary, is a small business centre, constructed in the early nineteenth century at the instigation of William Alexander Madocks, M.P. He had the mile-long embankment over the estuary of the Glaslyn constructed, thus reclaiming some 7,000 acres of valuable land and enabling the harbour to be built. The town has been laid out in keeping with its setting and is a picturesque place with marvellous views of Cardigan Bay and the Merionethshire hills. Its harbour has been of considerable importance to the slate industry of the region.

Three miles away is Portmeirion (37), certainly the most unusual village in Wales, for it is entirely Italianate in style. This, too, is the result of the efforts of one man, for its design was the work of the distinguished Welsh architect, Mr Clough Williams-Ellis. He set out to create a holiday village which would be free from the careless building which can detract from the natural beauty of a chosen site. Although the buildings are of differing styles, they harmonise quite successfully, and every year Portmeirion and its fine wild garden, 'the Gwyllt', attract many sightseers.

37

The long peninsula called the Lleyn is the most westerly part of Caernarvonshire and is an area of considerable beauty as well as of geographical and historical interest. The road which runs westwards from Portmadoc comes first to Criccieth (38). This is a pleasant holiday resort with lovely sands and enjoys a sheltered position on Tremadoc Bay. The town looks out over the Glaslyn sands and behind it the mountains of Snowdonia rise magnificently. Criccieth Castle, rebuilt in the thirteenth century by Edward I, looks down on the little harbour. Just over a mile from Criccieth is the little village of Llanystumdwy, where Lloyd George spent his boyhood, married, and was finally buried in a simple grave.

About eight miles to the west of Llanystumdwy is Pwllheli (39), the capital of Lleyn, which was granted its status of a free borough by the Black Prince in 1355. The name is generally taken to mean 'the saltwater pool', but some see it as a corruption of 'Porth Heli', the harbour of a lord called Heli. Once the harbour was more important than that of Caernarvon, but it became silted up and almost useless. In 1903, however, it was cleared of its debris and now provides pleasant shelter for fishing and pleasure craft. Four miles along the coast is the picturesque village of Llanbedrog (40), which has a superb beach and a rocky headland providing marvellous views. Near the extreme tip of the Lleyn is Aberdaron, called 'the most remote village in Wales'. From here the visitor may set out for Bardsey Island, which for hundreds of years was a place of pilgrimage.

On the other side of the peninsula is Nefyn (41), until recently a little fishing town, and now one of the loveliest resorts of the Lleyn. Nefyn has a long history: Edward I held a great tournament here in 1284 to celebrate his triumphs in Wales, and in 1355 Nefyn was created one of the ten royal boroughs in North Wales. To the north-east rise the peaks of 'the Rivals' where the remains of early fortifications are still to be seen.

38

40

41

Criccieth (38), station balnéaire plaisante, jouit d'une situation abritée sur la Baie de Tremadoc. Pwllheli (39) à environ neuf milles à l'ouest de Criccieth, est la capitale du Lleyn. Son port offre une situation plaisante pour les bateaux de pêche et de plaisance. A quatre milles de Pwllheli sur la côte se trouve le pittoresque village de Llanbedrog (40) qui possède une plage splendide. Nefyn (41) est une des plus jolies stations balnéaires du Lleyn et détient un passé riche car la ville fut un des dix bourgs royaux du Pays de Galles en 1355.

Criccieth (38) ist ein angenehmer Ferienort, der eine geschützte Lage an der Tremadocbucht genießt. Hinter Criccieth ragen die herrlichen Berge der Snowdoniagegend empor. Pwllheli (39) ist der Hauptort der Lleyn. Sein Hafen bietet Fischerbooten und Vergnügungsdampfern einen angenehmen Schutz. Vier Meilen der Küste entlang von Pwllheli liegt das mahlerische Dorf Llanbedrog (40), das einen herrlichen Strand besitzt. Nefyn (41) gehört zu den schönsten Ferienorten der Lleyn und hat eine lange Geschichte, wurde es doch im Jahre 1355 zu einer der zehn königlichen Städte von Wales gemacht.

Le Château de Harlech (42), qui date d'Edward I, détient une position romantique sur les falaises de la baie de Tremadoc. Les eaux du Lac Celyn (43), à quelques milles à l'est de Ffestiniog, traversent la vallée de Tryweryn et sont bordées de chaque côté par les montagnes Arennig. Au sud du Lac Celyn s'étend le Lac Bala (44), lac naturel le plus grand du Pays de Galles, qui fait presque quatre milles de long et un demi-mille de large. Les Chutes de Pistyll Rhaeadr (45) dans le Denbighshire sont peut-être les plus belles du Pays de Galles. A Carrog (46) la Rivière Dee traverse des collines vertes sous un pont pittoresque qui date de 1660. Sur son chemin vers Llangollen elle coule près du petit village de Glyndyfrdwy (47).

Schloß Harlech (42), zur Zeit Eduards des Ersten gebaut, liegt romantisch auf den Felsen ob der Tremadocbucht. Der See Llyn Celyn (43) bedeckt das Tryweryntal einige Meilen östlich von Ffestiniog. Südlich des Llyn Celyn befindet sich der Balasee (44), der mit vier Meilen Länge und einer halben Meile Breite der größte natürliche See von Wales ist. Der Pistyll Rhaeadr-Fall (45) in der Grafschaft Denbigh ist wahrscheinlich der prächtigste Wasserfall von Wales. Zwischen grünen Hügeln hindurch erreicht der Dee Carrog (46), wo er von einer schönen Brücke aus dem Jahre 1660 überspannt wird, und auf dem Wege nach Llangollen fließt er dicht an dem kleinen Dorf Glyndyfrdwy (47) vorbei.

42

43

44

45

46

47

Harlech, formerly the county town of Merioneth and now a village, lies on the perimeter of Snowdonia. Harlech's great glory is the castle (42) dating from the time of Edward I, built quadrangular in plan with round corner towers. Romantically situated on the cliffs overlooking Tremadoc Bay and enjoying magnificent views of the Snowdon range and the Lleyn, it has endured at least three sieges, one of which is said to have given rise to the famous song 'Men of Harlech'. Coleg Harlech ('Harlech College') was founded in 1927 and is regarded as one of the finest adult education centres. North-east of Harlech the waters of Llyn Celyn (43) cover the Tryweryn Valley, with the Arennigs on either side.

Bala, in north-east Merionethshire, is a charming town which was made a royal borough in 1324 by Edward II, and in the eighteenth century it was important in the Welsh woollen trade. Lake Bala (44), called Llyn Tegid in Welsh, is a very popular tourist attraction. It is the largest natural lake in Wales, being nearly four miles in length and half a mile wide. It is a popular sailing centre and Llanuwchllyn at the far end is a resort much favoured by fishermen.

Every mountainous country has fine waterfalls and Wales is no exception, but it is usually necessary to leave the main routes to discover the best of them. Perhaps the finest are the Pistyll Rhaeadr Falls (45) in Denbighshire where the water of the Disgynfa falls over 200 feet down the hillside in a succession of torrents, some four miles from Llaurhaiadr-yn-Mochnant.

On its course from Lake Bala to Llangollen the River Dee makes its way through much beautiful countryside. At Carrog (46) it passes under a fine bridge dating from 1660 and onwards close by the little village of Glyndyfrdwy (47). In the fourteenth to fifteenth centuries the lands around this village belonged to Owen Glendower, who waged war for fifteen years against Henry IV of England.

48

Llangollen (48) détient une situation privilégiée sur une étendue magnifique près de la Rivière Dee. Le canal de Llangollen (49) est tout proche du village de Trevor. Il était à l'origine utilisé pour transporter l'ardoise de la région de Llangollen. De nos jours il est utilisé par les estivants à la recherche de paisibles vacances sur l'eau. Le Château de Chirk (50) fut construit par Roger Mortimer sur des terres qui lui furent octroyées par Edward I. On pense que c'est dans le petit village d'allure originale d'Hanmer (51) qu'Owen Glendower fut marié à Margaret fille de Sir David Hanmer.

49

Llangollen (48) befindet sich inmitten einer wunderschönen Landschaft an einer herrlichen Strecke des Dee. Der Llangollen-Kanal (49) fließt dicht an dem Dorf Trevor vorbei. Der Kanal diente früher zum Transport des Schiefers aus der Llangollengegend; heutzutage aber gebrauchen ihn Urlauber. Schloß Chirk (50) wurde von Roger Mortimer auf Boden gebaut, der ihn von Eduard dem Ersten geschenkt worden war. Dieses Schloß wurde 1310 fertig gebaut. Im seltsamen kleinen Dorf Hanmer (51) soll sich Owen Glendower mit Margaret, Tochter des Sir David Hanmer verheiratet haben.

50

Llangollen (48) stands amid beautiful countryside on a magnificent reach of the River Dee. The name of the town is derived from St Collen, to whom the parish church is dedicated. Llangollen is famous for its 'Ladies' and their house. From the latter part of the eighteenth century until their death, Lady Eleanor Butler (d. 1829) and the Hon. Sarah Ponsonby (d. 1831) lived at Plas Newydd, a black and white mansion where they entertained many well-known people of their day, including William Wordsworth, the Duke of Wellington and Sir Walter Scott. Llangollen is also renowned for the International Eisteddfod which has taken place each year since 1947. Llangollen has never been a real centre of industry but during the late eighteenth to the early nineteenth century slates were quarried in the vicinity and transported by means of the Llangollen Canal. The canal (49) is now used by holidaymakers seeking a quiet time afloat.

The village of Chirk stands on the Oswestry–Llangollen road at the entrance to the Ceiriog Valley. Chirk Castle (50) above the village was built by Roger Mortimer on lands given to him by Edward I. It was completed in 1310 and has changed little in external appearance since that time. The castle contains many treasures of art and interesting portraits, and many of its rooms are open to the public.

The quaint little village of Hanmer (51), north-east of Chirk, is known for its association with Owen Glendower. It is believed that he was married here to Margaret, daughter of Sir David Hanmer, in the church that existed before the present beautiful building.

51

The Dolgoch Falls (52) on the Afon Dysynni, Merionethshire.
Les chutes de Dolgoch (52) sur la Rivière Dysynni, Merionethshire.
Der Dolgochfall (52) am Afon Dysynni, Grafschaft Merioneth.

Mid-Wales

Although Mid-Wales is a rather remote region it has amidst its great diversity of scenery much to offer the visitor. In this wildly beautiful area are to be found high hills, small mountains, gentle slopes and rocky crags, interspersed with moorlands and cut across by beautiful river valleys.

Perhaps the waters of Mid-Wales are the region's most remarkable feature. Throughout Mid-Wales are a number of man-made lakes, created by damming some of the larger rivers, to supply water for the larger English conurbations. Though commercial in purpose these lakes are magnificent and have brought further beauty to the wild valleys they occupy. Mid-Wales is also renowned for its spas which became fashionable in the late eighteenth and early nineteenth centuries. Llandrindod Wells, Builth Wells and Llanwrtyd Wells are among the best known, their waters containing salts which are of benefit in the treatment of certain diseases. These spas are attractive places and now make good centres for exploring the countryside around. Mid-Wales also has much fine river scenery, including the estuary of the Mawddach which is thought to present one of the best views in Europe. The valley of the River Teifi near Cardigan is among the finest in Wales and the river offers very good salmon fishing.

On the coast of Mid-Wales are many pleasant resorts, each with its own particular attraction. Barmouth is popular for its position on the marvellous Mawddach estuary, while Aberystwyth has many amenities and is a good centre for many excursions. Aberporth is delightfully secluded and New Quay and Aberaeron offer good sailing. Inland Mid-Wales is, however, largely an agricultural area with sheep farms and small market towns scattered across it. Much of the region is thinly populated, and although access by rail is limited there are good roads which bring the majority of places of interest within reach for the motorist. It is a particularly fine area for walking in, and if the visitor leaves the main routes there is much unspoiled beauty to be discovered.

The delightful resort of Barmouth (54) stands on the Merioneth coast in the Mawddach River estuary and is a splendid centre for exploring the magnificent scenery of the county on both sides of the Mawddach. Across the estuary reaches Barmouth Bridge, which carries a railway track and may also be used by pedestrians. It has been said that there is no finer scene in the whole of Europe than the view of the Mawddach estuary from this bridge. Barmouth is particularly popular for this 'sublime' estuary and the town's magnificent sands. Most of the present town of Barmouth is modern, although it has a long history and was once an important port. Llanaber Church, Barmouth's mother church and dedicated to St Bodfan, is almost two miles from Barmouth's present centre and dates from about 1200.

Before the Afon Mawddach (53) reaches its estuary and the sea, it flows close by the small town of Dolgellau, the capital of Merionethshire, which lies beneath the Cader Idris mountain. Dolgellau is an old town with the austere beauty of solid grey slate and stone architecture, with narrow winding lanes and backways. It was known to the Romans who made it the junction of three of their roads. Later it became an important market for the woollen industry of Wales, but today its fame chiefly rests on its superb situation, and the good fishing and magnificent scenery in the neighbourhood. The Precipice Walk (55) offers fine views over the Eden Valley and passes the remains of Cymner Abbey, a former Cistercian house, founded in 1199 by Gruffydd ap Cynan, the Lord of Gwynedd.

South-east of Dolgellau is the fascinating little village of Dinas Mawddwy, which takes its name from the River Mawddach. It lies among steep hills which stand close to one another, with only narrow valleys between them. This little village was the capital of Merionethshire until the reign of Henry VIII. The main road from Mawddwy to Dolgellau climbs over the Bwlch Oerddrws Pass (56) whose name means 'Cold Door Pass'. This reaches a height of 1,178 feet and then the road descends through open countryside with superb views of the Cader Idris range.

53

54

55

La Rivière Mawddach (53) traverse un paysage magnifique avant d'atteindre le fameux estuaire de Mawddach, spectacles des plus beaux d'Europe peut-être. Barmouth (54) se trouve sur la côte Merioneth dans l'estuaire de la Rivière Mawddach et forme un centre superbe pour explorer le magnifique paysage du comté de chaque côté de la rivière. Le Precipice Walk (55) près de Dolgellau offre des vues splendides sur la Vallée de l'Eden et passe près des restes de l'Abbaye de Cymner, ancienne demeure cistercienne. La grand-route de Dinas Mawddwy à Dolgellau grimpe la passe de Bwlch Oerddrws (56).

Der Afon Mawddach (53) fließt durch eine wunderschöne Landschaft und mündet zuletzt in die berühmte Mawddachbucht, die wahrscheinlich die prächtigste Ansicht ganz Europas bietet. Barmouth (54) liegt an der Küste der Grafschaft Merioneth an der Mawddachbucht. Die sogenannte „Abgrundwanderung" (55) dicht bei Dolgellau bietet schöne Aussichten über das Edental und führt an den Ruinen der Cymnerabtei, eines ehemaligen Zisterzienserhauses, vorbei. Die Landstraße zwischen Dinas Mawddwy und Dolgellau führt über den 1178 Fuß hohen Bwlch Oerddrwspaß (56) hinüber.

Between Dinas Mawddwy and Machynlleth lies the small town of Mallwyd. Very pleasantly situated on the River Dovey (57), known as the Afon Dyfi in Welsh, Mallwyd is particularly attractive to anglers. Cader Idris (58), 2,927 feet in height, lies to the south of Dolgellau. Its name means the 'chair of Idris' who was a mythical giant. As 'Idris' in Welsh is Arthur in English, it has been suggested that the legend surrounding the mountain may be associated with the Arthurian story. The northern side of Cader Idris is formed by almost perpendicular precipices but the slopes on the southern flank are gentler. From the summit the view is extensive and includes the great sweep of Cardigan Bay and the peaks of Snowdonia.

On the southern shore of the Mawddach estuary opposite Barmouth is the small village of Arthog behind which rises Tyrau-mawr, the westerly summit of the Cader Idris range. Eight hundred feet high above Arthog nestle two tarns, the Llynnau Creggennen, one of which is shown opposite (59).

The road leading southwards from Dolgellau runs down steeply through the Tal-y-Llyn Pass (60) to reach the beautiful lake of Tal-y-Llyn which lies on the southern foot of Cader Idris. At the far end of the lake is the tiny hamlet of Tal-y-Llyn (61), which gave the lake its name. There are marvellous views here of Cader Idris, and the fishing is good. Aberdovey (62) lies south-west of Tal-y-Llyn on the estuary of the River Dovey. Last century this was a port busy with foreign trade, but now it is a lovely holiday resort, popular on account of its fine setting and lovely sands.

57

58

59

La splendide rivière de Dyfi passe Mallwyd (57) entre Dinas Mawddwy et Machynlleth. Cader Idris (58), 2 927 pieds de haut, s'étend à quelques milles à l'ouest de Mallwyd. Son nom signifie la « chaise d'Idris », géant mythique. Sur sa face nord, à 800 pieds d'altitude, se nichent deux petits lacs connus sous le nom de Llynnau Creggennen (59). La grand-route qui mène au sud de Dolgellau forme une descente abrupte à travers la Passe de Tal-y-Llyn (60) pour atteindre le Lac de Tal-y-Llyn et le petit hameau du même nom. De là on a une vue splendide du Cader Idris (61). A l'estuaire de la Rivière Dovey, s'étend Aberdovey (62), une jolie station balnéaire.

Der bildschöne Afon Dyfi fließt an Mallwyd (57) zwischen Mawddwy und Machynlleth vorbei. Der 2927 Fuß hohe Cader Idris (58) ragt einige Meilen westlich von Mallwyd empor. Auf seiner Nordseite auf einer Höhe von 800 Fuß liegen zwei kleine Bergseen, die Llynnau Creggennen (59) genannt werden. Die Landstraße, die von Dolgellau nach Suden fuhrt, geht steil durch den Tal-y-Llyn-Pass (60) hinab und erreicht den bildschönen Tal-y-Llynsee und den kleinen Weiler Tal-y-Llyn. Von hier aus gibt es wunderbare Aussichten auf den Cader Idris (61). An der Mündung des Dovey liegt Aberdovey (62), ein reizendes Ferienörtchen.

61

60

62

Towards the end of the last century a water supply was provided for the great city of Liverpool by the creation in the heart of Montgomeryshire of a reservoir called Lake Vyrnwy (63). It was formed by damming the River Vyrnwy, and the 160-foot-high dam, nearly 400 yards long, encloses the largest lake in Wales, a sheet of water of over thirty-five square miles. The water is conveyed to Liverpool by an aqueduct seventy-five miles in length, the first two miles of which are tunnelled into the hillside. This principal reservoir of the Liverpool water supply was formed between 1880 and 1890, and holds 12,131 million gallons. There is little to show that this lovely lake is not entirely natural, and it has certainly added charm to the area. Another artificial lake, the Clywedog Reservoir (65), lies south of Lake Vyrnwy. The Clywedog Dam was built in 1968 across this tributary of the Severn, and helps to regulate the flow of the Severn. The reservoir has likewise brought beauty to an otherwise desolate area.

Some miles south-west of Lake Vyrnwy, not far from the boundary of Shropshire and Montgomeryshire, lies the town of Welshpool, which is called Trallwng in Welsh. For a long time it was an important market for the woollen industry. In the Powysland Museum there are many interesting exhibits, including relics of the twelfth-century Cistercian Abbey of Strata Marcella, some three miles away. One of the greatest attractions of Welshpool is, however, Powys Castle (64), which now belongs to the National Trust. Built of red sandstone, some of the castle dates from the late thirteenth century but much was added to it in the sixteenth. In the early nineteenth century the remarkable grounds were modified by Capability Brown.

The little town of Llanidloes stands some miles south-west of Welshpool at the confluence of the Severn with its larger tributary the Clywedog. Once lead mining was one of the main industries of the area, and then it became an important centre for the weaving of wool. It still produces wool and also leather work. Perhaps the most distinctive feature of the town is the Old Market Hall (66), a Tudor half-timbered building of 1609. It is now a museum.

63

64

65

66

Le réservoir immense, le Lac Vyrnwy (63), fut créé à la fin du siècle dernier pour alimenter Liverpool en eau. Une des attractions de Welshpool est le Château de Powys (64), dont certaines parties datent du 13e siècle. Un autre lac artificiel, le réservoir de Clywedog (65) se trouve au sud du Lac Vyrnwy, et a conféré une certaine beauté à une vallée autrement désolée. Un des traits des plus distincts de la ville de Llanidloes est le Vieux Bâtiment du Marché (66) construit en 1609.

Der Vyrnwysee (63) wurde Ende des letzten Jahrhunderts als Reservoir für die Stadt Liverpool aufgestaut. Einer der größten Reize des Welshpools ist Schloß Powys (64), welches zum Teil aus dem 13. Jahrhundert stammt. Ein zweiter künstlicher See, das Clywedog-Reservoir (65), liegt südlich vom Vyrnwysee und hat einem sonst öden Tal einen gewissen Reiz verliehen. Die bemerkenswerteste Sehenswürdigkeit der Stadt Llanidloes ist die 1609 gebaute Alte Markthalle (66).

Aberystwyth (67) se trouve au confluent des eaux du Rheidol et de l'Ystwyth, et est à la fois une station balnéaire et une ville universitaire. Du chemin de fer, qui va de Aberystwyth au Pont du Diable, il y a des vues splendides; parmi celles-ci le « Cerf blanc » (68), cicatrice curieuse provoquée par les essais de mine dans le flanc de la montagne. Non loin de là on peut voir le barrage de Cwm Rheidol (70). Le Pont du Diable se trouve dans un paysage magnifique et tout près on peut voir la splendide Rivière Ystwyth (69). A un demi-mille du « Cerf Blanc » sont les Chutes de Rheidol (71), et tout près, le Mynach (72) descend le long d'un abîme rocheux en une série de cataractes.

Die Stadt Aberystwyth (67) befindet sich am Zusammenfluß des Rheidol und des Ystwyth und ist sowohl ein Ferienort als auch eine Universitätsstadt. Prächtige Aussichten bietet die Bahnlinie von Aberystwyth nach der Teufelsbrücke. Dazu gehört diejenige auf den Cwm Rheidol-Damm (70) und auch den ,,Weißen Hirsch" (68), eine merkwürdige Spur, die durch ehemalige Schürfarbeiten nach Blei an der Bergflanke verursacht wurde. Die Teufelsbrücke liegt inmitten einer wunderbaren Landschaft, und dicht dabei kann man den herrlichen Fluß Ystwyth (69) sehen. Jenseits des ,,Weißen Hirsches" ist der Rheidolfall (71), und nicht weit davon fließt der Mynach (72) in einer ganzen Reihe Katarakte den felsigen Abgrund hinab.

67

68

69

70

71

72

The seaside town of Aberystwyth (67), Cardiganshire, situated almost at the centre of the curve of Cardigan Bay where the waters of the Rheidol and the Ystwyth meet, is both a holiday resort and a university town. Although the core of the University College of Wales (founded 1872) is the neo-Gothic hotel built by Thomas Savin about 1860, the main university buildings lie on the hills overlooking the town. To be found here also is the National Library of Wales, which was completed in 1955 and opened by the Queen. The Library shares with five others in the British Isles the privilege of receiving a copy of almost every new book published in this country, and it houses a wonderful collection of Welsh books, documents and manuscripts. Aberystwyth also has a ruined castle which was built during the reign of Edward I, a small harbour and a pleasant beach.

A well-known excursion from Aberystwyth is by the narrow-gauge railway to Devil's Bridge, about twelve miles away amid a magnificent, romantic landscape. Seven and a half miles from Aberystwyth along the track is Aberffrwd, which is the nearest station to the Cwm Rheidol Dam (70). Also close to Aberffrwyd can be seen the 'Stag', a curious scar caused by trials for lead in the mountainside (68). From Aberffrwyd the engine pulls the train up a very steep gradient towards Devil's Bridge Terminus, passing Rheidol Falls (71), beyond which the gorge is particularly splendid. At Devil's Bridge, from the roadway opposite the hotel, there is a marvellous view of the Mynach Falls (72), contained in the grounds of the hotel, where the Mynach cascades down to join the Rheidol. At the point where the roadway crosses the river, Devil's Bridge itself can be seen, actually consisting of three bridges, built one on top of the other. It is thought that the first bridge on this site was constructed by monks in the eleventh century. South of Devil's Bridge the River Ystwyth (69) flows through fine scenery on its journey to Cardigan Bay.

73

74

75

Les eaux de la Rivière Elan ont été endiguées de façon à former quatre barrages qui alimentent Birmingham en eau. Le réservoir le plus au nord est celui de Craig-yr-Allt-Goch. Celui de Craig Goch Dam (73), contient 2 028 millions de gallons. Au sud de ce dernier est le réservoir de Pen-y-Garreg (74), qui contient 1 332 millions de gallons. Au sud de Pen-y-Garreg se trouve le réservoir de Careg-ddu (75). Le viaduc de Careg-ddu (76) forme un passage plein d'attrait au-dessus du réservoir. En dessous de Careg-ddu se trouve le réservoir de Caban Coch.

Mit vier prächtigen Dämmen hat man am Elan Stauseen geschaffen, welche die Stadt Birmingham mit Wasser versorgen. Der nördlichste davon heißt der Craig-yr-Allt-Goch-Stausee, und der Craig Goch-Damm (73) ist 513 Fuß lang und 120 Fuß hoch. Südlich davon liegt der Pen-y-Garreg-Stausee (74). Sein Damm ist 528 Fuß lang und 123 Fuß hoch. Südlich von Pen-y-Garreg befindet sich der Careg-ddu-Stausee (75). Der Careg-ddu-Viadukt (76) bildet einen sehr reizenden Übergang über diesen Stausee. Unter Careg-ddu liegt der Caban Coch-Stausee. Sein Damm wurde 1892 als erster der Serie gebaut.

Towards the end of the nineteenth century the need for water in the industrial Midlands led to the construction of a series of dams in the area known as the Elan Valley on the borders of Radnorshire and Breconshire. On their way from the source on the moorlands south of the Plynlimon range to join the Wye at Rhayader, the waters of the Elan have been dammed to form four artificial lakes which store water for Birmingham and which extend over 1,000 acres. The mighty dams which hold back the water are over 100 feet high and their heavy grey stone blends well with the landscape. The lakes behind them are magnificent, particularly when full after rain, and are a great tourist attraction. Despite their commercial purpose they certainly enhance rather than detract from the beauty of the region. This set of dams was begun in 1892, officially opened in 1904 by Edward VII, and completed in 1907. The most northerly of the reservoirs is the Craig-yr-Allt-Goch Reservoir, which holds 2,028 million gallons of water and covers over 200 acres. The Craig Goch Dam (73) is 513 feet long and 120 feet high. South of this lies the Pen-y-Garreg Reservoir (74), which holds 1,332 million gallons. The Pen-y-Garreg Dam is 528 feet long and 123 feet high. Careg-ddu Reservoir (75) nestles below Pen-y-Garreg and the Carreg-ddu Viaduct (76) makes an attractive crossing of this reservoir. Below Carreg-ddu is the Caban-Coch Reservoir, whose dam was the first-built of the series.

After the Second World War the Claerwen Dam, built of concrete, was constructed to dam the branch valley of the Claerwen, and was completed in 1952. The dam, which was opened by Queen Elizabeth II, is the largest of the series and holds back a 600-acre lake.

The countryside surrounding the lakes consists of hills and crags, some of which reach the 2,000-foot level, and the highest part of the valley becomes wild, open and bare. Several sheep farms were submerged when the reservoirs were built, including Cwm Elan House where Shelley stayed in 1811 and Nantgwllt where he stayed in 1812. Motoring is easy in this beautiful area, and the whole district is a tribute to the skill of the engineers who envisaged and carried out the project.

76

77

Après la deuxième guerre mondiale la Rivière Claerwen (77) fut aussi endiguée. Au-dessus du barrage la rivière va rejoindre la Rivière Wye près de Rhayader, et dans cette contrée (78) on peut trouver quelques-uns de paysages les plus sauvages du centre du Pays de Galles. A quelques milles au sud de Rhayader est Llandrindod Wells; son voisinage (79) est renommé depuis longtemps pour la valeur curative de ses eaux. A partir de Rhayader la Rivière Wye (80) descend vers le sud vers Builth Wells. Le magnifique pont (81) qui traverse la rivière à cet endroit remonte au 18e siècle.

Nach dem zweiten Weltkrieg wurde der Claerwen (77) auch gestaut. Unterhalb des Dammes fließen seine Gewässer weiter und münden endlich in den Wye ein; die Umgebung (78) gehört zu den wildesten Landschaften ganz Mittelwales. Südlich von Rhayader liegt Llandrindod Wells, deren Umgebung (79) für den medizinischen Wert seiner Quellen berühmt ist. Von Rhayader fließt der Wye (80) gegen Süden nach Builth Wells, einst wegen seiner medizinischen salz- und schwefelhaltigen Quellen bekannt. Die prächtige Brücke (81), die den Fluß hier überquert, stammt aus dem 18. Jahrhundert.

The River Claerwen (77), whose dam was opened in 1952, unites with the Elan and then flows on to join the River Wye near Rhayader. Some of the wildest scenery in central Wales is to be found in the neighbourhood of Rhayader (78) and is extremely attractive for walkers and geologists. The town of Rhayader is called in Welsh 'Rhaeadr Gwy', which means 'the waterfall of the Wye'. Situated in a hollow beside the River Wye and surrounded by rocky slopes, it was once an important fortress and later a manufacturing centre. Now it is a pleasant market town, noted for its sheep farms and fine fishing facilities. Nothing remains of the twelfth-century castle, probably built by Rhys ap Gruffyd, but there are some old houses and the church still has its Norman font. The construction of the great reservoirs in the area certainly brought renewed vigour to the town.

A few miles south-east of Rhayader is Llandrindod Wells, close to the junction of the Ithon and Aran Rivers. The neighbourhood (79) has long been well known for the medicinal value of its waters, but it was not until the late eighteenth century that the thirty wells were made use of as a health resort. Now Llandrindod Wells is the county town of Radnorshire and a popular international resort, both as a health spa and an excursion centre. From the surrounding countryside there are fine views of the mountains beyond the Wye.

From Rhayader the road south follows the River Wye which joins the River Irfon in a charming glen and comes to Builth Wells, once well known for its medicinal saline and sulphur waters. The river (80) is here the boundary between Radnorshire and Breconshire. The bridge that crosses it at Builth (81) is magnificent with six arches and dates from the eighteenth century. Builth is a busy old town, and is a marvellous centre for exploring this varied region of Wales. The remains of an early Norman motte and bailey castle, which was partly destroyed in 1260 by Llewelyn ap Gruffyd, can still be seen although little remains of the stone castle built later on the same site by Edward I in the late thirteenth century.

78

79

80

81

82

83

A six milles au sud de Builth Wells la Wye (82) rencontre la
Rivière Edw près du charmant petit village de Aberedw. La
route de Builth Wells vers Brecon traverse la Duhonw au
« Pont Blanc » dans Llanddewi'r-cwm (83). La Rivière Irfon
(84) coule vers le sud de sa source et passe Llanwrtyd Wells,
une jolie petite station balnéaire. Il y a un certain nombre
d'autres stations balnéaires charmantes sur la baie de Cardigan
au nord de la Rivière Teifi. Aberaeron (85) a un nom qui vient
de la rivière, laquelle descend dans une belle vallée pour se
jeter dans la mer à cet endroit. New Quay (86 et 87) est con-
struite en terrasse sur une haute falaise qui fait face au port.

Sechs Meilen südlich von Builth Wells mündet der Edw in der
Nähe des Dorfes Aberedw in den Wye (82) ein. Die Straße
zwischen Builth Wells und Brecon überquert den Duhonw über
die Weiße Brücke bei Llanddewi'r-cwm (83). Der Irfon (84)
fließt von seiner Quelle südwarts an Llanwrytd Wells, einem
herrlichen Ferienort, vorbei. Es gibt viele andere reizende
Ferienorten an der Cardiganbucht nördlich vom Teifi. Aberaeron
(85) erhielt seinen Namen vom Fluß, der von den Bergen durch
ein prächtiges Tal hinabfließt und an dieser Stelle in das
Meer einmündet. New Quay (86 und 87) besteht aus Häuser-
zeilen, die von einem Felsen auf den Hafen hinunterblicken.

84

85

Six miles south of Builth Wells the Wye (82) runs through steep hills and is joined by the waters of the Edw. Here is to be found the lovely village of Aberedw. Its beautiful church has an ancient wooden roof and a fifteenth-century screen, and above the village stand the ruins of an ancient castle, the seat of the last Llewelyn. The main road from Builth Wells to Brecon crosses the River Duhonw at Llanddewi'r-cwm (83), not far from the little church originally built in the seventeenth century. The River Irfon (84) runs southwards from its source on Bryn Garw past Llanwrtyd Wells, once a spa and now a beautiful village holiday resort offering good fishing and golf.

North of the estuary of the Teifi are a number of delightful resorts on Cardigan Bay. Among these is Aberaeron (85). It derives its name from the river which comes down through a beautiful valley to enter the sea at this point. The town was laid out and built to a planned pattern in the early nineteenth century and is delightful. At the end of the nineteenth century it was a fishing port, but now the harbour is almost entirely used by pleasure craft. New Quay (86 and 87), another of these resorts, began to grow up in the eighteenth century as a fishing port. Built on terraces on a high cliff overlooking the harbour, it is becoming more and more popular as a holiday resort, especially for a sailing holiday. There are several interesting caves in the cliffs, and colonies of sea birds are often to be seen on a rock to the west of the town. A little way to the east of New Quay is Llanina Church, one of the smallest in Wales.

87

88

89

90

Aberporth (88), au sud-ouest de New Quay le long de la côte, est un charmant petit village de pêche et une station balnéaire populaire. A Cardigan, qui se trouve près de l'embouchure de la Rivière Teifi et qui fut autrefois un important port de mer, un somptueux pont (89) traverse la rivière. En amont de Cardigan on arrive à Cenarth, qui s'étend des deux côtés de la rivière et possède un magnifique vieux pont (91) et des chutes pittoresques (90).

Aberporth (88), südwestlich von New Quay, ist ein schönes Fischerdorf und ein beliebtes Ferienort. In der Stadt Cardigan, die an der Mündung des Teifi und früher ein wichtiger Seehafen war, überquert eine schöne Brücke (89) den Teifi. Stromaufwärts von Cardigan kommt man nach Cenarth, das an beiden Flußufern gebaut ist und eine schöne alte Brücke (91) und einen mahlerischen Wasserfall (90) besitzt.

Aberporth (88), south-west along the coast from New Quay in a secluded position, was an important port in the seventeenth century. Standing on cliffs above two sandy coves, it is now a lovely fishing village and a popular holiday resort. Its romantic scenery also makes it a favourite with artists.

Just under four miles to the north of Cardigan, Mwnt is now in the care of the National Trust. The tiny whitewashed church below the hill is at least 600 years old and probably replaced an earlier chapel. Cardigan (89), whose Welsh name is Aberteifi, stands near the mouth of the River Teifi. Here a fine arched bridge crosses the river, and makes a good viewpoint. This pleasant town has a long history. In its earlier days Welsh princes lived here, and the town remained Welsh until the twelfth century when it was taken over by Norman invaders; later it became an English borough. Little remains of the ancient castle which was a fortress until it was captured by Parliament during the Civil War. It is claimed that the church was founded as early as the fifth century. The present building has a tower dating from the early eighteenth century. In the eighteenth and nineteenth centuries Cardigan was an important sea port, but silt has formed a bar at the river mouth and it is used only by smaller craft. Two miles north on the north bank of the Teifi is Gwybert-on-Sea, where salmon are netted by methods which have changed little over the passing centuries.

The Teifi Valley is thought to be one of the finest in Wales, and the river is one of the best Welsh rivers for salmon fishing. Upstream from Cardigan is Cilgerran, with fine remains of a thirteenth-century castle perched high on a rocky eminence overlooking the river. Cilgerran Church has an interesting stone in the churchyard with inscriptions in Ogam and Latin. Continuing upstream we come to Cenarth, one of the most charming points on the river. The village stands on both sides of the Teifi and has a fine old bridge (91). It also has picturesque falls up which salmon leap (90). Cenarth is one of the few places where coracles are still used, though the construction of these ancient British boats is a dying art.

Kidwelly Castle (92), Carmarthenshire, was first built in the early twelfth century.
Le Château de Kidwelly (92), dans le comté de Carmarthenshire.
Schloß Kidwelly (92), Grafschaft Carmarthen, stammt aus dem 12. Jahrhundert.

South Wales

Like the rest of Wales, South Wales has a beauty that is wide and varied. Industry is very important here due to the area's great mineral wealth, and because of this there are twice as many inhabitants as in the rest of Wales. The industries have, however, only scarred a small part of the region, remaining confined principally to the large ports of Cardiff and Swansea and the mining towns of the Rhondda. Yet even in those places the landscape has kept some of its original majesty, and close by there are areas as attractive as any other part of Wales.

The scenery of South Wales is less dramatic than that of North Wales for it lacks a mountain mass comparable with Snowdonia. However, it does have fine mountains in the Brecon Beacons, which rise to nearly 3,000 feet. They lie at the centre of the Brecon Beacons National Park, a mountainous area of unspoiled countryside, and command wide and interesting views. South Wales is less remote than Mid-Wales and lacks some of the wild beauty, but it does have its own large share of fine characteristics. Among these are the great areas of hill and moorland, as in Breconshire and Carmarthenshire, the picturesque river valleys, such as that of the Usk in Monmouthshire, and the romantic glens such as the Vale of Neath in Glamorganshire. Many regard the real glory of South Wales as the Gower Peninsula, with its grand limestone cliffs and magnificent beaches. Along this and the western coast there are charming holiday resorts, and inland there are others, each with its particular attractions.

South Wales is rich in history and scattered all over the region are many interesting relics of settlements long since past. Ruined castles are so numerous in South Wales that the region has come to be known as 'the country of castles'. Also in the region is St David's Cathedral. South Wales is a highly accessible area with much to offer the holidaymaker as well as many features to attract naturalists, botanists, geologists, walkers and mountaineers, and has facilities for many sports.

Fishguard (93) était autrefois un petit port de pêche sur la mer et maintenant la ville est devenue le terminus des bateaux irlandais vers l'Irlande du sud. La Tête de Saint David, Pembrokeshire, est tournée vers l'ouest, dans l'Atlantique et en dessous de la Tête s'étend la Baie de Whitesand (94). Le petit village de St David est classé parmi les villes de cathédrale. Vue de l'extérieur la Cathédrale de Saint David (95) a un aspect sombre, mais l'intérieur est plein de beauté. Solva (96) le long de la côte de St David est un charmant village; ce bras de mer sert aux petits bateaux de pêche et de plaisance.

Fishguard (93) war früher ein kleiner Seehafen und ein Fischerstädtchen und ist heutzutage der Ausgangshafen für die Fähren nach Südirland. Das St. Davids-Vorgebirge, Grafschaft Pembroke, erstreckt sich nach Westen in den Atlantik, und darunter liegt die Whitesandbucht (94). Das kleine Dorf St. Davids wird zu den Domstädten gezählt. Von der Außenseite sieht der Davidsdom (95) etwas düster aus, aber drinnen ist er voller Schönheit. Solva (96), nicht weit von St. Davids an der Kuste gelegen, ist ein reizendes Dorf, und die kleine Bucht wird von kleinen Fischerbooten benützt.

93

94

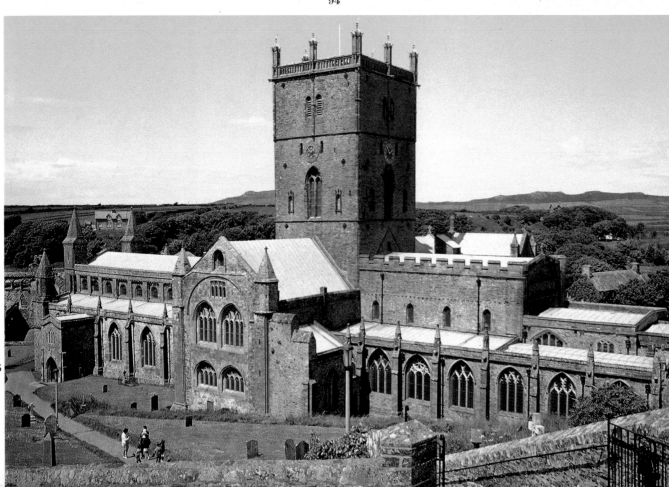

95

Fishguard (93), called Abergaun in Welsh, lies under the slopes of Mynydd Preseli overlooking Fishguard Bay. Once a little seaport and fishing town, it is now a modern port and the terminus for the Irish boats to Eire. On the Goodwick side of Fishguard Bay are the quays and the Irish Ferry terminal, under the heights of Pen Caer. The breakwater which runs out half a mile to sea was built in 1907 and protects the modern harbour. Fishguard makes a good centre to visit many of the other interesting places in the area.

St David's Head, Pembrokeshire, reaches westwards into the Atlantic and is named after the saint who did most to establish Christianity in the sixth century in Wales. The shape of this rock outcrop is very similar to that of the western end of the Lleyn peninsula in the north. The Head forms the northern side of the bay called in English Whitesand Bay (94) and in Welsh Porthmawr or 'the great bay'. This is a beautiful place with wild flowers in season growing on the headland. Close by Whitesand Bay can be seen the ruins of the ancient little Chapel of St Patrick, where Irish pilgrims used to bring offerings, and on the headlands around are many traces of occupation by prehistoric man.

The little village of St David's stands in a windswept plateau on the promontory which forms the northern arm of St Bride's Bay. This small place ranks as a cathedral city, for after the death of the patron saint in 601 it became a centre of pilgrimage and eventually the site of a cathedral (95). William the Conqueror, Henry II, Edward I and Queen Eleanor all visited the shrine. From the outside the cathedral has a somewhat sombre look, but the interior is full of beauty. The intricate roof, made of Irish oak, and the beautiful fourteenth-century screen are but two of many features of interest.

Solva (96), just along the coast from St David's, was once a small, flourishing port, but now the inlet is used by pleasure craft as well as small fishing boats.

97

98

99

100

St Bride's Bay, which stretches for almost ten miles, is named after St Bride or Bridget, the fifth-century saint. This is a rather remote but certainly beautiful bay, with sandy stretches and flower-covered cliffs. At the southern end of the bay are the small villages called Broad Haven (97) and Little Haven (98), both of which are pleasant holiday resorts. Broad Haven has magnificent sands and offers very good bathing. Little Haven occupies an inlet south of Broad Haven, and was once an important harbour. It now offers good facilities for sea fishing. The charming village of Angle (99) lies on the peninsula at the southern side of Milford Haven, between the two bays, Angle Bay and West Angle Bay. The village has only one street, and close by there are the fragments of an old castle. In the churchyard of the much restored Angle Church is a small chapel thought to have been founded in the fifteenth century.

The East Cleddau River flows into the north of Milford Haven and the main road from Narberth to Haverfordwest crosses this river by Canaston Bridge. Not far from the bridge stand the moated ruins of Llawhaden Castle, once one of the palaces of the bishops of St David's. These ruins date mainly from the fourteenth century, and consist of a rectangular court and angle towers. The castle was robbed of its lead roofing in the sixteenth century. Now in the care of the Department of the Environment, the castle has been renovated and may be visited. Llawhaden Church (101), prettily situated beside the river and below the castle, was rebuilt in the late fourteenth century but retained much of the earlier Norman work. Its main tower is situated at the south of the nave with a lower and smaller embattled tower attached to its south side. South-west of Llawhaden stands Picton Castle (100). It is believed to have been first built by William de Picton during the reign of William II and as such to be one of the oldest residences in Wales. During the Civil War it was held against the forces of Parliament. On the east side of Picton Park is Slebech Park, where there are the picturesque ruins of the Church of the Knights Templar. To the south Picton Park extends to the estuary of the East Cleddau.

Sur la Baie de St Bride reculée mais pleine de beauté on peut trouver les stations de Broad Haven (97) et de Little Haven (98). Broad Haven est un petit hameau avec des plages magnifiques excellentes pour les bains. Little Haven s'étend sur une crique étroite juste au sud de Broad Haven et offre de bonnes facilités pour la pêche en mer. Le charmant village de Angle (99) se trouve sur la péninsule au sud de Milford Haven et n'a qu'une seule rue. L'église de Llawhaden (101) a une belle situation au côté de l'East Cleddau qui finalement se jette dans les eaux de Milford Haven. Au sud-ouest de Llawhaden est le Château de Picton (100), construit à l'origine par William de Picton sous le règne de William II.

An der eher etwas abgelegenen, dafur umso schöneren St. Bridesbucht sind die Seebäder Broad Haven (97) und Little Haven (98) zu finden. Broad Haven ist ein kleiner Weiler mit ausgezeichneten Stränden, die gute Bademöglichkeiten bieten. Little Haven liegt in einer engen Talmulde unmittelbar südlich von Broad Haven und bietet gute Möglichkeiten zum Seefischen. Das reizende Dorf Angle (99) liegt auf der Halbinsel südlich von Milford Haven und hat nur eine Straße. Die Llawhadenkirche (101) befindet sich in einer schönen Lage am Ufer des East Cleddau, der schließlich bei Milford Haven ins Meer einmündet. Südwestlich von Llawhaden liegt Schloß Picton (100), das von William de Picton gebaut wurde.

101

Pembroke is dominated by its castle (102), which has been most skilfully restored and is an impressive fortress. The first Norman castle was twice burned down, but the round keep, built at the beginning of the thirteenth century, still stands. It is seventy-five feet high and about sixty feet in diameter, and the walls at the base are about twenty feet thick. Beneath the ruins of the Great Hall is a natural cave, known as the 'Wogan'. The castle was almost completed by the end of the thirteenth century, and it figured prominently in the Civil War, finally surrendering to Cromwell's forces.

Carew Castle (103), on a creek some four miles north-east of Pembroke, was begun in the second half of the thirteenth century, but much of it was reconstructed in the late fifteenth and early sixteenth century. Carew is also well known for its ancient cross of Celtic design, which probably dates from the ninth century, and for its medieval church where members of the Carew family are buried.

About six miles south-east of Pembroke stands the village of Manorbier, overlooked by the shell of Manorbier Castle, which dates from the late thirteenth century. Manorbier Church is of similar age although additions were made in the fifteenth century. The village enjoys a very pleasant situation, and has a sandy beach in a little bay (104). Manorbier was the birth-place in 1146 of the medieval historian, Giraldus Cambrensis, whose works include *Itinerary through Wales*. Close by Manorbier is Lydstep Haven (105), a lovely bay with an interesting view of Caldey Island. The island belongs to a priory of Cistercian monks who came to the island in 1929. Caldey has a long history as a monastic island, for it is believed that the first monastery founded here was a Celtic one of the sixth century. A Benedictine monastery was founded here in 1113 and some of its buildings survive. The lighthouse (106) dates from 1828.

102

103

Pembroke est dominé par son château (102) qui date du 13e siècle. Il a été adroitement restauré et forme une forteresse impressionnante. Le Château de Carew (103) sur une crique à quelques milles au nord-est de Pembroke, fut commencé dans la deuxième partie du 13e siècle, mais la plus grande partie fut reconstruite fin du 15e siècle début du 16e. A environ six milles au sud-est de Pembroke se trouve le village de Manorbier, surmonté par la carcasse du Château de Manorbier, qui date du 13e siècle. Le village jouit d'une position agréable et possède une plage sablonneuse sur une petite baie (104). Tout près de Manorbier est Lydstep Haven (105), une charmante baie avec une vue intéressante sur l'Ile de Caldey. L'île appartient au prieuré des moines cisterciens qui vinrent s'installer en 1929. Le phare (106) date de 1828.

Pembroke wird von seinem Schloß (102) beherrscht, das aus dem 13. Jahrhundert stammt. Es ist auf geschickte Art restauriert worden und ist heutzutage eine imponierende Festung. Schloß Carew (103) liegt einige Meilen nordöstlich von Pembroke an einer kleinen Bucht; es wurde in der zweiten Hälfte des 13. Jahrhunderts ursprünglich gebaut. Ungefähr sechs Meilen südöstlich von Pembroke liegt das Dorf Manorbier, worauf die Ruinen des aus dem Ende des 13. Jahrhunderts stammenden Schlosses Manorbier hinabblicken. Das Dorf besitzt einen Sandstrand an einer kleinen Bucht (104). In der Nähe von Manorbier liegt Lydstep Haven (105), eine herrliche Bucht mit einer interessanten Aussicht auf die Insel Caldey. Diese gehört einer Probstei von Zisterziensern an, die 1929 auf die Insel kamen. Der Leuchtturm (106) stammt aus dem Jahre 1828.

The charming little town of Tenby (107), a few miles above Manorbier on the Pembrokeshire coast, is perhaps the best-known resort of the area. The history of Tenby dates back to at least the ninth century when it was a Welsh stronghold. It was captured by the Normans, and by the late thirteenth century a castle crowned the headland between the North and South Sands and a wall was built around the town. The castle and walls still survive today. In the seventeenth and eighteenth centuries Tenby was a port, and in the early nineteenth century became a fashionable watering place. Many of the elegant houses and much of the atmosphere of that time are preserved today.

East of Tenby, Carmarthen Bay stretches towards the Gower Peninsula. The coastal road first comes to Saundersfoot, a pleasant seaside village with an interesting coastline and long stretches of sand (108). This is a popular resort especially with yachtsmen, for whom the harbour (109) offers a convenient anchorage. About three miles beyond Saundersfoot the tiny village of Amroth (110) lies by the sea, which comes dangerously close in winter. Amroth Castle is comparatively modern, a late eighteenth-century castellated house, where Lord Nelson stayed in 1802. Some four miles further on is Pendine (111), where some of the pioneers of motor racing came to attack speed records on the magnificent sands. An interesting detour brings the visitor to Laugharne (112) on the right-hand estuary of the Taf. Here can be seen a romantic castle, originally of the twelfth but rebuilt in the fourteenth century.

107

108

109

La petite ville fortifiée de Tenby (107) était au tout début du 19e siècle une ville d'eau à la mode dont il reste encore de nombreuses demeures élégantes de cette époque. A l'est de Tenby la route côtière passe d'abord Saundersfoot, un village au bord de la mer avec de longues étendues de sable (108) et un port (109) qui offre un mouillage commode. A environ trois milles de Saundersfoot le minuscule village d'Amroth (110) se trouve à proximité de la mer. Quatre milles plus loin est situé Pendine (111), où les pionniers de courses de moto vinrent ici établir des records de vitesse sur les espaces sablonneux. A Laugharne (112) on voit un romantique château de 14e siècle.

Das reizende ummauerte Städtchen Tenby (107) war im frühen Teil des 19. Jahrhunderts ein beliebter Badeort und besitzt immer noch viele der eleganten Häuser aus jener Zeit. Östlich von Tenby kommt man nach Saundersfoot, einem angenehmen Dorf am Meer mit langen Sandstränden (108) und einem bequemen Hafen (109). Nach weiteren drei Meilen erreicht die Küstenstraße das kleine Dorf Amroth (110), welches nahe am Meer liegt. Vier Meilen weiter liegt Pendine (111), auf dessen prächtigem Strand einige Pioniere des Motorsports Rekorde aufstellten. Bei Laugharne (112) steht ein romantisches Schloß aus dem 14. Jahrhundert.

110

111

112

The Gower Peninsula, often called 'the Land of the Setting Sun', lies to the west of Swansea, being bounded on the north side by the estuary of the River Loughor, the Bury Inlet. In extent it is comparatively small, reaching some fifteen miles west from Swansea, but it is so very different in character from the adjoining mainland of South Wales that the peninsula has become very popular as a holiday centre. The glory of Gower is its southern coast, a succession of bays and coves, each with its own special character. Rhossili Bay (113) at the western end of the peninsula has nearly three miles of sand. The village of Rhossili consists of a few houses grouped around the thirteenth-century church of St Mary. Rhossili enjoys fine scenery, and the Worm is now a nature reserve. The islands of Worms Head reach out for about a mile into the Bristol Channel and are separated from the Worm at high tide.

Porteynon lies east of Rhossili, and is a lovely old fishing village with thatched cottages and narrow lanes nestling in a cove, and the bay is protected to the west by Porteynon Point (114). On the west side of this point is the curious cave, Culver's Hole, which may well have been used by smugglers in days gone by. Another delightful village is Oxwich, which lies close by Three Cliffs Bay (115) where the Pennard stream runs into the sea. Remains of a Norman motte lie near this bay, and this area is well endowed with caves. The ruins of Pennard Castle, built in the thirteenth century, stand on the dunes behind the bay. Caswell Bay (116), still further east, has magnificent sands and at some points pine trees grow close to them. A seaside path leads from Caswell across to Langland Bay (117). This is a busy area, with hotels and new building developments beyond the fine sands. Mumbles Head (118) reaches out at the western side of Swansea Bay in the form of two islands. On the outer island stands the lighthouse, first built in 1794.

113

114

115

La Baie de Rhossili (113) à l'extrémité ouest de la péninsule Gower s'étend sur presque trois milles de sable. Porteynon se trouve à l'est de Rhossili et est un charmant petit village de pêche avec des maisonnettes aux toits de chaume qui s'ancrent dans l'anse de la baie. La baie est protégée à l'ouest par Porteynon Point (114). Un autre charmant village est celui de Oxwich qui se trouve tout près de la Baie des Trois Falaises (115), à l'endroit où le cours d'eau Pennard se jette dans la mer. Un chemin le long du rivage mène de la Baie de Caswell (116) à la baie de Langland de l'autre côté (117). C'est là un endroit populaire, où les hôtels et bâtiments neufs s'élèvent au delà du sable côtier. A l'est de la Baie de Langland, Mumbles Head (118) s'étend en forme de deux îles. Sur celle la plus éloignée s'élève le phare, construit d'abord en 1794.

Die Rhossilibucht (113) am westlichen Ende der Gowerhalbinsel hat einen fast drei Meilen langen Sandstrand. Porteynon liegt östlich von Rhossili und besteht aus einem lieblichen alten Fischerdorf, dessen Strohdachhäuser sich behaglich an eine kleine Bucht schmiegen. Die westliche Seite der Bucht wird von der Porteynon-Landspitze (114) geschützt. Ein anderes entzückendes Dorf der Gegend heißt Oxwich, das ganz dicht an der Dreifelsenbucht (115) liegt, wo der Bach Pennard ins Meer einmündet. Noch weiter östlich kommt man von Caswellbucht (116) auf einem Küstenweg zur Langlandbucht (117). Dies ist ein beliebter Ort, und es gibt Hotels und Neubauten hinter dem schönen Sandstrand. Östlich von der Langlandbucht erstreckt sich das Mumbles-Vorgebirge (118), wo der im Jahre 1794 erbaute Leuchtturm steht.

119

120

121

122

Swansea, the county borough of the county of Glamorgan, is situated where the River Tawe falls into Swansea Bay. It is the second largest city in Wales and has a very marked dual nature. The eastern side of the city is entirely industrial, and within about a twenty-mile radius are many types of factories and works, and also the docks and a flourishing port: But on the western side is the handsome Swansea, of which the hub is the Castle Gardens (119). Modern buildings surround these gardens on three sides while the old castle forms a part of the fourth. This is not the original Norman structure but the remains of a fortified manor house built by Henry Gower, Bishop of St David's in about 1340. Singleton Park (120), originally the seat of Lord Swansea, is now the site of University College, one of the four colleges of the University of Wales. Not far from the centre of the busy city are Swansea's fine sands and Swansea Bay, always popular with the small-boat enthusiasts.

Some sixteen miles north of Swansea, away from the busy main road, is the quiet Carmarthenshire hamlet of Trapp. From Trapp a narrow road leads to one of the most remarkable castles in Wales, Carreg Cennen Castle (121). Perched on a height of almost 900 feet, with a steep incline on one side and on the other a 300-foot precipice falling to the River Cennen, it occupies a very impressive site. The castle dates from Norman times although the present building is thought to have been constructed during Richard II's reign. Perhaps the most interesting feature of this castle is the 150-foot-long passage carved through the rock of the cliff face to a cistern and lit by openings cut in the cliff face.

About eight miles north of Trapp, in the hills north of Llandeilo, is the village of Talley. Here lie the ruins of a Cistercian abbey founded in the twelfth century beside two small lakes which gave it the Welsh name of Tal-y-Llychau ('Head of the Lakes'). One of these peaceful lakes is shown above (122). About sixteen miles east of Trapp the River Mellte flows by the village of Ystradfellte, whose name means 'way over the River Mellte'. Nearby on this river can be seen some magnificent falls (123).

Swansea est la seconde ville du Pays de Galles et présente une nature double bien marquée. Le côté est de la ville est entièrement industriel, alors que le côté ouest est celui du Swansea élégant dont le centre est occupé par les « jardins du château » (119). Le Parc de Singleton (120) est sur l'emplacement du collège universitaire. Près du village de Trapp est le Château de Carreg Cennen (121), construit sous le règne de Richard II. Plus au nord le village de Talley est à proximité de deux petits lacs, dont vous pouvez voir l'un ici (122). A environ seize milles de Trapp la Rivière Mellte traverse le village de Ystradfellte et à proximité on peut voir de magnifiques chutes (123).

Swansea zeigt einen ganz auffallenden dualistischen Charakter. Die Industrie liegt in der östlichen Stadthälfte, und die westliche Hälfte, das schöne Swansea, wird vom Schloßgarten (119) beherrscht. Die Universität liegt im Singletonpark (120). In der Nähe des Dorfes Trapp steht Schloß Carreg Cennen (121). Auf einem fast 900 Fuß hohen Hügel steht das Schloß, welches unter der Regierung Richards des Zweiten gebaut worden sein soll. Das Dorf Talley liegt in der Nähe von zwei kleinen Seen, wovon einer (122) hier gezeigt wird. Ungefähr sechzehn Meilen östlich von Trapp fließt der Mellte am Dorfe Ystradfellte vorbei, und in der Nähe ist ein prächtiger Wasserfall (123) zu sehen.

123

Merthyr Mawr (124), se trouve tout près de l'embouchure de la Rivière Ogmore. Au sud-est de Merthyr Mawr est le village de St Donat, mieux connu pour son château (125), siège de la famille Stradling du 13e au 18e siècle. Le Château de Caerphilly (127) est le deuxième plus grand château après celui de Windsor, et fut construit au 13e siècle. Le Château de Cardiff (126) fut commencé à l'époque des Normands, et plus tard agrandi en une forteresse magnifique.

Merthyr Mawr (124), ein mahlerisches Dorf mit Strohdachhäusern, liegt nahe an der Mündung des Ogmore. Südöstlich davon befindet sich das Dorf St. Donat, wohlbekannt durch sein Schloß (125), welches einst den Sitz der Familie Stradling bildete. Schloß Caerphilly (127) ist neben Windsor das größte Schloß Großbritanniens und wurde im 13. Jahrhundert gebaut. Schloß Cardiff (126) wurde zur normannischen Zeit begonnen und später zu einer prächtigen Festung ausgebaut.

124

125

126

Merthyr Mawr (124), a picturesque village with thatched cottages, stands close to the mouth of the River Ogmore. The village dates back to at least the ninth century, but traces of what is thought to have been a Neolithic settlement have been found in Merthyr Mawr Warren. About seven miles south-east of Merthyr Mawr is St Donat's village, best known for its castle (125), the seat of the Stradling family from the thirteenth until the eighteenth century. In the twentieth century the castle was bought by the late Mr Randolph Hearst, the American newspaper owner. He restored and altered the castle, which contains much of beauty and interest, including carvings by Grinling Gibbons and a room with a copper ceiling.

Caerphilly Castle (127), north-east of St Donat's, was built here in the thirteenth century and is second only in size to Windsor. This great fortress follows the concentric plan which was used by Edward I in so many of the castles in North Wales, and was almost impregnable. In the fifteenth century the masonry was allowed to decay and it was not until some thirty years ago that restoration was begun. The most remarkable feature of the building is the leaning tower which tilts nearly ten feet out of the vertical. This was caused by the demolition of an adjoining tower during the seventeenth century.

Cardiff, on the banks of the Taff where it runs into the Bristol Channel, has a long history. During the first century AD the Romans established a military station here, and there was enough building surviving for the Normans to use as a nucleus for the first Cardiff Castle. This began as a simple motte and bailey, but as time passed it was enlarged to form a formidable fortress (126). It still has its Norman keep and moat, and parts of the Roman wall can still be seen. South of the castle in Cathays Park, once part of the castle grounds, at the beginning of the present century was laid out one of the finest civic centres in the British Isles. The 200-foot-high tower of the City Hall is the focal point of the Civic Centre. The building, in Renaissance style, contains a council chamber, an assembly hall and an impressive marble hall. Other public buildings surrounding Alexandra Gardens are the Law Courts, the National Museum of Wales, the Temple of Peace and the University College of South Wales and Monmouthshire, one of the four constituent colleges of the University of Wales. Just over two miles to the north-west is Llandaff Cathedral, which has been much restored, although the See dates from the sixth century.

En 1957 un espace, d'une grande beauté et de paysage varié s'étendant sur de nombreux milles dans le Breconshire, le Carmarthenshire et le Monmouthshire fut destiné au Parc National de Brecon Beacons. Les Brecon Beacons (128) qui occupent une position centrale dans cette région sont les plus hautes montagnes du sud du Pays de Galles. La Rivière Usk, qui apparaît au nord du Parc, coule en direction du sud et traverse un paysage campagnard d'une grande beauté comme celui de Crickhowell (130). Le Parc National offre de nombreuses et belles promenades dont une emmène le visiteur aux Chutes de Blaen-y-Glyn (129). Un paisible canal va de Brecon à Newport, en passant par Govilon (131).

1957 wurde ein landschaftlich außergewöhnlich schönes und abwechslungsreiches Gebiet, das sich über mehrere Quadratmeilen der Grafschaften Brecon, Carmarthen und Monmouth erstreckt, zum Brecon Beacons Nationalpark ernannt. Der Usk, der seine Quelle im Norden des Parkes hat, fließt am Fuße der schönen Breconhügel (128) vorbei und windet sich langsam in südöstlicher Richtung durch eine reizende Landschaft (130 – der Usk bei Crickhowell). Der Nationalpark offeriert zahlreiche schöne Wanderungen, wie zum Beispiel diejenige, die den Besucher an dem Blaen-y-Glyn-Wasserfall (129) vorbeiführt. Ein friedlicher Kanal führt von Brecon über Govilon (131) nach Newport.

128

130

129

131

In 1957 an area of great beauty and variety of scenery covering 381 square miles in Breconshire, 87 square miles in Carmarthenshire and 51 square miles in Monmouthshire was designated the Brecon Beacons National Park. This park, part of the uplands of Wales, offers its visitors a peaceful and largely unspoilt countryside. Contained in this area are red sandstone mountains and moorlands, limestone foothills and crags cut across by lush river valleys and deep gorges. The Brecon Beacons (128), which occupy a central position in the area, are the highest mountains in South Wales, the loftiest peak being that of Pen-y-Fan (2,907 feet). The River Usk, which rises in the north of the Brecon Beacons Park, follows a winding and beautiful course through the park until it reaches the Bristol Channel after its long course of fifty-seven miles. On its way it flows through Brecon, a prosperous place dominated by its magnificent cathedral.

On the northern side of Brecon stand the ruins of Brecon Castle, believed to have been built in about the eleventh century by Bernard de Newmarch. The Usk flows on, past the foot of the Brecon Beacons, in a south-easterly direction through much beautiful countryside, such as that near Crickhowell (130), between Brecon and Abergavenny. Crickhowell is a pleasant little town, on and around a hill. There is a bridge with several arches across the Usk, and the remaining fragments of a castle. In the Brecon Beacons National Park there are many marvellous walks to be made to explore the mountains, forests and moorlands. One such walk south of Brecon in the Tal-y-Bont Forest takes the visitor past the Blaen-y-Glyn Falls (129), and climbs above the falls and the farm to reach the ridge of Craig Fan-Ddu (2,224 feet), from which there are marvellous views. A peaceful canal, now used by those in search of a quiet, lazy holiday, leads from Brecon to Newport. There is a particularly pleasant walk alongside the canal from Govilon (131), close by Abergavenny, to Gilwern, attractively situated at the entrance to the Clydach Valley.

132

Non loin de la Rivière Usk se trouve le village de Raglan, connu par les ruines de son château (132) lequel remonte en grande partie du 15e siècle. Grosmont est une petite ville originale située près de la Rivière Monnow près de la limite du Herefordshire. Le château actuel (133) fut construit au tout début du 13e siècle en même temps que les châteaux de White et de Skenfrith pour monter la garde sur la Vallée d'Or. Skenfrith (134) est à proche distance de Grosmont. Son église du 13e siècle présente un clocher pittoresque. A Monmouth le portail fortifié du 13e siècle sur le pont de la Monnow (135) est unique en Grande-Bretagne. La vieille ville marché de Chepstow (136) jouit d'une position splendide près de la Rivière Wye.

Unweit des Usk liegt das angenehme Dorf Raglan, welches wegen der Ruine eines aus dem 15. Jahrhunderts stammenden Schlosses (132) berühmt ist. Das seltsame kleine Städtchen Grosmont liegt auf einem Hügel beim Fluß Monnow nahe der englischen Grafschaft Hereford. Das heutige Schloß (133) wurde im 13. Jahrhundert gebaut, um das „Golden Valley" (das goldene Tal) zu beschützen. Skenfrith (134) liegt nicht weit von Grosmont. Seine aus dem 13. Jahrhundert stammende Kirche hat einen mahlerischen Turm. Das aus dem 13. Jahrhundert stammende Tor auf der Brücke über den Monnow in Monmouth ist einmalig in Großbritannien. Die alte Marktstadt Chepstow (136) genießt eine prächtige Lage am Wye.

A few miles south-east of Crickhowell lies the pleasant village of Raglan. This place is famous for its ruined castle, one of the finest of medieval strongholds. The present castle (132) was built largely by Sir William ap Thomas in the mid fifteenth century, and his son, William Herbert, Earl of Pembroke, made many additions. This is believed to be the last example of medieval fortification in Britain.

Grosmont, Monmouthshire, is a quaint village lying on a hill by the Monnow River not far from the Herefordshire border. Its present castle (133) dates mostly from the early thirteenth century with some additions in the fourteenth. It was built to mount guard over the Golden Valley, along with White and Skenfrith Castles. Now only a quiet village, Grosmont was very important during the Middle Ages.

Skenfrith, a short distance from Grosmont, lies in the valley of the Monnow River. The castle, dating from the thirteenth century, consists of a four-sided outer fortification, guarded at each corner by a round tower, and inside a small circular keep on a slight mound. The church (134) dates mostly from the thirteenth century and has a picturesque, square, double-roofed bell tower. It contains the famous Skenfrith cope of about 1500. Monmouth, once the county town, is a quiet little market town attractively situated on the bank of the Wye where the Monnow flows into it. The famous thirteenth-century gateway on the bridge over the Monnow (135) is unique in Britain.

The old market town of Chepstow (136) is set on the hillside on the right bank of the River Wye. Its magnificent castle, dating mostly from the thirteenth century, occupies an area of almost eleven acres. Best seen from the iron bridge crossing the Wye, it is a splendid first view on entering Monmouthshire.

133

135

134

136

137

Close to the River-Wye, in green meadows with wooded hills all around, stands Tintern Abbey (137). The abbey was originally founded in 1131 by Walter Fitz-Richard, Lord of Striguil, for monks of the Cistercian order from Cîteaux in France, but the existing ruins are from a later date. About 1220 a great rebuilding scheme was begun. The monastic buildings were first constructed, to meet the needs of the brethren, and then the rebuilding of the church was begun in about 1270. The church was consecrated in 1288, but was not completed until about 1320. Although roofless now, the church is a magnificent blend of Early English and Decorated architecture in a very good state of preservation. Delicate foliage has made its home in the nave, and the lovely windows encompassing the views of wooded hills add to the delights of Tintern Abbey. All is beautiful here, providing a fitting finale for our short visit to Wales.

L'Abbaye de Tintern (137), peut-être une des plus belles ruines cisterciennes de Grande-Bretagne, se dresse près de la Rivière Wye dans des prairies vertes entourées de collines boisées. Ces ruines remontent au 13e siècle.

Die Tintern-Abtei (137), wahrscheinlich eine der schönsten Zisterzienserruinen Britanniens, steht nahe am Wye in grünen saftigen Weiden, umgeben von bewaldeten Hügeln. Diese Abtei stammt aus dem 13. Jahrhundert.

© Copyright 1973 Jarrold and Sons Ltd, Norwich. 85306 456 3
Published and printed in Great Britain by Jarrold and Sons Ltd, Norwich. 173